Love and Errors

by Kimberly Dark

Published by Puna Press
P.O. Box 7790, San Diego, CA 92167
www.punapress.com

Cover art "Dynamic Messaging" by Samantha Fields

Cover design Toni Le Busque
tonilebusque.com

Printed in the United States of America
by EC Printing
ecprinting.com

Thank you.

Library of Congress Control Number: 2018930267

ISBN: 978-0-9983728-1-5

For my son, Caleb James Dark Westberg, who endured countless poetry slams, readings, demonstrations and events as a child so that I could learn to write poetry. His questions, wisdom and social engagement are still helping me learn to be a better parent.

Table of Contents

Love and Errors

Love and Errors: Nothing But

When all is told and done, there's nothing more
than regret for what we've poorly wrought, our
errors, and the thoughtful penance done for
hurting others. All that matters really
is to learn to right a wrong, meet an eye
that judges, prompting judgment of oneself.
And then to let the judging rest, take on
the lessons, build the habits of redress.
To come to see there's nothing more beneath
the wounds and wrongs than sorrow and to learn
that love alone should take its rightful place
to teach the heart, so it need never yearn
for others' praise, forgiveness and grace.
Peace comes from all around to fill this place.

Belonging

Cat's behaving strangely
lying underneath the chair
rather than up on it.
I do not have a name for her;
she isn't mine. Still, my home
is where she chose to live.
I accept that I am hers
(I wonder what she calls me.)

Her position's no proof
of poison though I think
about it nonetheless.
Breath comes easy –
mine and hers, not so
the tenants in the eaves
whose anguish I have
felt these past few nights
then days as well, as I
look up and feel remorse
for even sleep is lost before
the sweet release of death.

I dream of people packed
in ships then barred from shores
crossing land that no one loves
the space between – or squeezing
in the cities' press, with hope to be
extruded – toothpaste-like from
from the tube of one nation
to the industrious brush of another.
I dream of mammals returning
to our inert states, we hairy

sacks of enriched water; what will
the carrion beetle call me?

The cat must keep from the dying
rats and so she does; they're in the eaves,
she with comfy sofas down below.
It's not as if we use that space above.
It's just their noise and habits that offend.
I prayed for them to leave the poison
even as I placed it.
This makes it seem they had a choice.
So they did, as well did I.
So do we all in moving, staying,
praying, loving, breathing,
in battle and in touch.

Dying, not so much.

Girl Wood

I could've broken like kindling
when he struck me
with his angry flint
but I know better than to let
him see my woody nature.
My job is to be supple,
a soft body trained as
landing pad.

I'm just fifteen
but you wouldn't know it.
People think they know
what numbers look like
how age equates wisdom,
save exceptions; an imagined
sophistication behind the eyes
They're wrong of course.
People make of looks
what culture tells them.
No rings around the trunk
or waist, or neck or eyes
to count and know how
one should treat a girl:
like a human, woman or child.

If I have been trained as
a landing pad, feel like
a bunch of kindling, then
my boyfriend is formed
for free fall, full of spark.
His body doesn't fill like mine –
with metaphor – until it becomes
nothing but meaning, nothing but
labels and choices and appearances and –
I'll tell you a secret.

I love the way my body feels.
Sex makes me curious
because there may be more
to my pleasure
than what I already know.
I could be wrong.

I'm like every other girl.
I worry about how I look
from every angle.
My hands are pretty, graceful
and seductive, I think; my calves
are nice. I wonder
if appearing to enjoy
his mouth on my skin
will make me seem too –
well, you know how the
seeming and sounding become
being and circumstance for a girl.
I notice my hand lifts to cover
my mouth; I don't want to
say anything aloud.
Still, my own voice
enhances my pleasure.
Except for worries,
soft sapling wood of me, wondering.

My boyfriend hit me
for the first time this morning;
I felt first heat,
then swelling. Saw his face
relax, his jaw go slack,
eyes icy, then empty
like he'd just landed
in something really soft, lush,
unbreakable.

Dating, Honesty

Once you've seen the bad stuff,
relief comes. The ones who
keep it hidden will cause trouble.
(That's what you tell yourself.)
Cat in bag, shoe un-dropped; wait.
It's always going to be something.

The quicker you hear the story
of the last lover who got a fist,
kitten drowned in the toilet,
sea of alcohol, acres of pills,
hungry, angry need of that body
seated before you, of whom
you want to make a noble story –

If they can talk about it, it's all
going to be okay, isn't that right?
The past is the past, and honesty
is sweet and promises relief,
like a drug itself,
when you're trying to avoid
that feeling of deserving
what's coming to you.

Sewing is Generally Taught by the Mother

She sleeps more soundly
now I've grown.
The needle is sharp.
I pierce the skin with ease,
pull my experience through,
tug her history back
into me. I tried to find the door
first; don't think I wanted
blood. I knocked and bruised
my knuckles knowing
I'd find an easy opening
or make another way.

Don't think me brutal for
taking up the sewing kit,
embroidery hoops and
tatting hooks; I know these
tools. My grandmother
introduced me. I tried
to read her skin, by then
she looked like sheets of
music, but I wasn't taught
to play or sing; too late
to learn before she
withdrew her offerings.

Mother I still have; I know
how to make, embellish
and I need what I need so I sew,
so I sew while she sleeps,
my skin, into my mother's
skin, pulling and wiping,
pressing taught and bunching.

If she wakes, I'll sew her
mouth shut as well. Closing
that wound is benevolent
and there's nothing more
for me to learn from her
anyway. We need our bodies
close and connected. We need
skin on skin, blood mixing into
the graft, nothing superficial.
It wasn't simple when it
started. I tore her open and
I will find the way back
whether it matters to her or not.
This wasn't my first choice.
I didn't start out for blood.
I knocked and cried out
but I couldn't find a way in.

Gender Certainty

Sometimes I'm not sure what gender a person is
so I have to turn my head, take another look.
I have to pause, look closely, see for myself.
It's important to know for sure.
Isn't that what we're taught?
I have to start a conversation, have an interaction,
try to understand.

Sometimes I need to make a date, go to dinner,
learn some more.
I need to find a private place,
peel off my clothes, meet some skin and feel it out.
I need to settle down for a while,
have children, pass some holidays, make rituals,
shed some tears, see some tragedies unfold.
I smile a lot, make meals, make love, take it all in,
go on trips, sleep close…

Sometimes I'm not sure what gender a person is
so I have to take the time to find out.

Resignation to Fashion

*"The thing at the moment is Adele. She's a little too
fat, but she has a beautiful face and a divine voice."*
Karl Lagerfeld, Coco Chanel designer

Mr. Lagerfeld, please accept my resignation
and my renunciation, as long as I'm at it.
You're not the boss of me;
I will not be working for you any longer.
As if you ever paid me!
As if I ever received health benefits
mobility benefits, or vacation time
from the idea that my body owes something
to the business of fashion, the cut of fabric,
the embellishment of jewels and metals,
plastic, glass and crepe, paint and wood.
I will take pleasure in these things now only
to serve my own attraction to color, texture, light.
I will not be working for you anymore.

I find myself working for you in odd moments –
standing on a street corner tugging to right a hem
or pulling a blouse lower over my belly
or feeling a shoe pinch as I walk, wondering
if I should've taken a taxi even though it's a nice
day.
Coco just wanted to be more comfortable,
so she snipped and sewed,
somehow, eventually, made you.
She took a simple hat and left it lovely.
This I understand; she wanted to ride a horse
in pants that let her breathe and she wanted to
carry a few things in an easy-to-grasp bag.
I would've measured, stocked and couriered for
these aims

but I will not be working for either of you anymore.
She is dead, and you are old, but so famous.
That's why I'm letting you know.
Fashion is no longer my religion,
though it's how my parents raised me.
I never felt fully spirited in worship
though I learned more than the basics:
how to spot the pious, the gifted, the talented,
how to shame the outcasts, convert the willing,
give charity to the needy.

I was raised to count my blessings, hide my flaws,
to worship the artful concealment of human
diversity
in favor of careful image and restraint.
So this is a renunciation of faith as well.

I realize that you can go on functioning without me,
so my resignation may not mean
to you what it means to me –
reclaiming my life and
my comfort *and*
my beauty.
Because I have noticed that the way a body looks
best
is in use, in movement. Yes, a body of any type, of
any size
is glorious in service of a will, a breath, and a mind
that loves.
I think you are the charlatan, sir, if you believe
you can call a body or a face imperfect
because you have failed to learn to adorn it
with grace, ease and care.

Yours beautifully, busily, on about my own
business,
Resigned

The Story He Can Understand

"Let me talk to him," I said to her
as the officer walked around to her side of the car.
A busy road on a hillside –
the kind that would wash out in a bad storm,
send little tin shacks tumbling,
foul people's drinking water for weeks.
To our left, the ravine and barbed wire fences
that separate the nation and city of my birth
from the nation we are in.

We were driving too fast,
though offense is not entirely necessary
for being stopped in this border city
by notoriously corrupt police.

Who will he be?

Police are people – different and changing.
I watch his face, jaw, stance.
He is looking at our car –
a good sign.
This is not personal.
He is trying to decide
based on the age, condition and value of the car
what our bribe will be.

"Buenos Dias!"
I lean across the seat, begin in a cheery tone.
He will get money
but I will try to maintain control of this interaction.

She sits beside me.
I send her a telepathic message:
Please stay quiet
take no offense
make no offense.
Let me handle this.

What negotiation could I make with her in these
quick moments?
I can but will her silence, hope she has nothing to
say.
While we are both foreigners,
I have more experience with this culture than she.
And I know enough to be a little frightened for us
both.
No. No time for that. I am vigilant for us both.
I am managing both of them in this moment.

He wants to speak English, ask questions.
Talk is good and I am warm, friendly, apologetic –
still speaking Spanish because she doesn't.
She must not join this conversation,
reveal herself as a threat to his fragile gender.

And this interaction is going well.
My focus is that all of us seem like nice people
with stories he can understand.
Simple stories keep us human.
Things are going well and yet,
how often is vigilance the order of the day for
women?
It doesn't matter whether the possible events
are only in my head today, rather than his.

Their possibility lives in my body memory –
always a certain tension in the body of one
who must read others
in order to stay safe.

I am managing.
He is managing.
She is sitting quietly
and this is not always so.

She is a great storyteller!
A big presence in the room,
she lives boldly – when we're on our home turf, at
least.
In the city, never hesitates to offer me her arm
when we are walking on the street.
She opens doors for me and
publicly accepts a quick kiss of thanks
for her common chivalry.
She is good at managing things too –
the glances of onlookers, the reinterpretation as man
and woman
no, woman and woman.
Dyke and woman? No. Man? No. Well.
She knows how to manage a situation too, no doubt.

One night in Denver, for example
we went in search of the perfect martini.
And this quest led us away from queer-only bars
into the Friday night urban press of a string of
upscale libationers.
I still can't recommend Denver's best martini
but we laughed a lot and I fell in love with her
again,

the evening barely tarnished by a near incident
involving our queerness.

In our joy, we sat close and spoke intimately,
as many couples do in a bar, warmed by a few
cocktails
but our kind are not always allowed intimacy.
At one point, sitting in a booth facing the door
she leaned me back for a proper kiss
and one of two men walking by stopped to stare.
Loudly he said, "Well what the hell do we have
here?"
His tone was menacing, drawing in the attention of
others,
not our kind.

Without pause, she delicately unhanded me,
grew to take up all the space around us and slowly
she stood, leading with her shoulders,
steady eye contact with the menacer she said
"Is there some kind of problem?"
The speaker hardened, bristled, but his buddy
(not wanting to waste a Friday night, perhaps)
said "No problem here. None at all!"
And moved his friend along.
She resumed her position next to me, hand on my
knee,
asked if I'd like another drink.

Next to me, in Tijuana, the officer staring in the
window
I am the woman with the story he can understand.
She is still big and strong and powerful
and I'm grateful that she is not acting that way now.

I'm not sure she knows that this negotiation
could turn at any moment.
I would be out of this car
and letting him press against me, cop a feel
as we negotiate my payment.
To protect her I would let him put me in my place
if it came to that.
My desire to protect her is at least as fierce
as her desire to protect me.
I love her
and I will not end up in a Mexican jail today
watching her beaten and gang raped
because she is a threat to maleness
and I need to be shown the error of my ways.
Women like her get the worst of it
but I have survived abuses,
avoided many others,
by managing the situation.

I am smiling at him
and keeping the conversation moving.
I am answering questions about the car, a husband,
my profession.
I know the right answers and she is letting me give
them
until he asks her occupation.
Does she understand that he is not truly interested?
He is considering our collective financial abilities –
and she is proud.
Knows the word for "firefighter" in many languages
and things are going so well, the conversation
almost jovial.
I don't think she really understands what is

happening here.
She has never left the United States before this trip,
taken at my urging –
let alone traveled to countries where machismo
rules –
where the male gender is an ever-fading mark
that must be re-inscribed many times a day
and women's blood is the ink.
She's never learned of countries,
such as this one,
where being gay is not defined
by the gender of the person with whom you have
sex
but by the role you take in the fucking.
And women never do the fucking.

I understand that this man's identity is a fragile
glass bauble.
I can see right through him.
I will be careful with him
because we are not getting cut today.
God help you if you seem to take male privilege
unduly!
And oh, my lover, you take it so well…

As she offers the Spanish word for firefighter –
a male-only job in this country, nearly so in our own –
I chuckle and
(still speaking Spanish so that her machismo
remains intact)
I reframe her as a paramedic
explain that in our country the two travel together
and that women aren't paid much anyway.
I am steering us back to the cost of the bribe

and she does not know that I have just insulted
her profession and accomplishments.
He does not have any idea,
as I haggle the bribe, pay the money, drive away
that she is
my lover.

That evening, safely at home in bed, she was gallant
once more,
back in her element,
she took me a little more aggressively than usual –
joyful at being back in a position she could
command.

As she started to form the clever and funny story of
the event
as she is wont to do,
I stopped her and said, "Thanks for letting me do
the talking today."
To which she replied, somber for a moment.
"I was scared."
I nodded and then made light of the situation again,
because I couldn't stay with my own fear.
I love her bigness and would not diminish her for
anything.
Masculinity is too fragile, no matter who's wearing
it, it seems.
And the truth is, we keep each other safe
even though she's the one who walks by the street,
as she offers me her arm.

Love and Errors

I probably could've thrust
the stick into his belly to
scramble away, but for what?
More men in the next room.
I keep it by the bed since we
are waiting for soldiers.
I woke before he was on me
and that's also why I didn't
use the stick; I saw his face.
He was not frightened, there
to do his job. He did not see
himself, but I saw him:
so young, my son's age, no.
Younger than my children.

Some women fight, some beg,
then there is violence.
It's not that I felt only love;
there was fear, but complex,
fear for both of us and I
shook my head, no, no, no.
Do not do this thing to us.
Even if I could not be your
mother but especially because
I could, I shook my head, no.

And as though from a corner of
the room, though also still me
I watched him hit me on cue,
felt strength in his shoulder,
the small bones in my neck
jostled as the muscles strained

to hold my head, lip bleeding,
swelling, I watched his method,
practiced, aloof yet angry son.

"Do not do this thing to us."
I said as he unzipped his pants,
Penis dirty, bloody, flaking, who
knows what. I wanted to clean him,
foolish child, this is an error.

He took my wet eyes into his
cold eyes briefly, then he
hit me again and the penis
went hard. It's not personal,
the body knows what it
practices and my body crouched,
a response to which he
was accustomed; the body folds
in danger and he had practiced
how to unfold such a body
for raping. I heard myself
sobbing, yes, for both of us.

My son, your body is not
a weapon. Retrieve it and
hold it with some dignity.
It is as precious as
the body from which you came.

After Five

It is after five p.m., so I lock the outside door.
There are two stalls so it's normally left open.
I lock it because it's after
five.
I notice the sole of her foot, turned strangely
from where I sit in the small stall.
She is in the larger wheelchair-accommodating stall
lying against the wall.

I approach
carefully,
push the door open with two fingers.

       "Are you okay?"
I say tentatively.
As I move forward,
I can see she is not.
Her body is twisted, legs spread,
one out behind her at an angle.
Her long burlap-colored skirt is filthy
and a little blood stained.
I can see only part of her face.
She is young.
She is alive.

She looks at me without moving her head.
       "Honey, can you move?"
I kneel tenderly beside
her.
I don't dare disturb the space around her with a
touch.
       "Can you talk to me?"

"Puede hablar espanol?"
Her voice is first gravely and low.
From screaming perhaps?
I have not heard anything from my office,
maybe 100 yards away.
A voice can be strained from being quiet too,
I think in these quick moments.

"Si, puedo." I respond.
Puedes movar las piernas?"

She has not moved yet.
Her face is pressed against the tile wall.
She is alive.

"It hurts to move."
I am at first confused by her English.
She adds,
"I want to know I can trust you."
She looks at me from the corner of her eye.

"You can trust me."

I sit close to this wounded child.
She is young.
She is alive.
Her head falls into my waiting lap.

"I should go for help.
You need help."
I say softly.

"No." She says.
"Me voy a morir."

"You're not going to die."
What makes me so sure?
Just that I am not dead?

I can often tell when a girl's been raped a year ago
just by looking at her.
This has been less than an hour ago, I'm sure.

"How old are you, mija?"
I smooth her hair.

"Fifteen."
Her voice is a high whine and
the mucous rises in her throat,
her nose, her eyes.
But no tears come.
She is young.
She is alive.

"You have to tell someone."
I stroke her head.
"It will be okay. You need help."

"I can't tell my family.
They would find out if I go to a doctor."

"You can't stay here in the bathroom either."

"You could stay with me." She says quickly
She is young.

"You're hurt, mija.
How do you know your family will be mad
at you?"

There is a silence.

"Who did this to you?"

"My brother." She whispers.
"And his friend." She adds with a small
shrug.

As she shifts in my lap, I see she is still bleeding.
I am shocked – afraid I have hesitated too long.
I look around for her blood in the stall.
No blood on the walls.

"How did they hurt you, honey?"
I lift her skirt a little.
Welts are already raised on her upper thighs.

"They didn't beat me up or nothing."
She says in defense.
"It's cause I fell trying to get away.
They just had sex with me."
She is pained in her attempt to move away from me.
"But with their fists too, you know?"

"Yes, I know. I'll be right back with some
help, okay.
I'll stay with you then."
I try to get up but she doesn't move.
She is limp in my lap.

"I won't be here."
She says defiantly into my leg.

"You can survive this." I say softly.

"I'll drown myself in that toilet." She says.

"You will still be here."

"No." She says.
She is young.
She is alive.

Anything but the whole history of ourselves is gone.
Adolescent girlhood in a bathroom.
Rape, abortion, vomiting, cutting.
This is adolescent girlhood in a bathroom.

I am overwhelmed by my memories,
yet anchored here by my age,
responsible to this moment
where I am a caring adult.

But the ghost of my self,
adolescent girl in a bathroom,
wails around my head.
I breathe deeply,
look at the ceiling,
let it enter my body.

"You will still be here."
I sigh.
"Porque ya estoy aqui."

I test the silence.
"I tried to kill myself in a few bathrooms too
when I found out
my body was worth less than garbage
crumpled and stained on a bathroom floor.

Better to end it than see my puffy face
in the mirror when I stood up.
Because I thought I was nothing.
But I was young.
I was alive."

She is quiet.
I continue.
Porque ya estoy aqui.
And because she is here too.
   "I kept my mind busy with higher thoughts
   while he hurt me.
   Sabes que, for me it was my step-father.
   Has your brother hurt you like this before?"

   "Not this bad."
Her voice is firmer, a little angrier.
I nod.

   "You can see that I am still here.
   Verdad, mija?
   And I'm not lying to you.
   I am okay.
   I am okay."

It is nearly six thirty when the ambulance
arrives.
I cradle her in the sound of my voice
while I wash her face with paper towels and cool
water.
The bleeding has stopped.
I loan her some lipstick
because she doesn't want to look ugly.

"Too pink."
She sticks out her tongue at the tube
right before they get here.

"Oh, I didn't bring it for you, chica!"
She laughs.
Checks again as the sirens come close.

"You gonna stay with me and talk to my
mom, right?"
I nod.
"You gonna talk to my dad?"

I nod again,
kiss her forehead.
I add,
"This still won't be easy for you.
And I'm so sorry for that."

Rest
(for Mollie and Mary)

I'm old enough that
they've started killing
my children – not just
my friends. It's not
enough that we
survived, if they
don't.

Two girls shot in
a park; one lives
asking through her
faceless face
about the other.
These lovers were
younger than my
children; they are
my children.

This is not
the way of things.
I have survived
them, and so
I must have
failed them. The
world has not yet
made a place of
love for my children
My life is comfortable,
but I don't rest well.

It seemed enough
to stay alive, live bold,
show the small-minded
bigots what love is – we
thought that was enough.
I have not yet
done enough.
Two girls at a picnic
table in the park
were not safe in their
gender, sex or beauty,
race or language -
I can't know what
ugly a shooter found
to take one child's
face, another's life.
I can't know what
pain was soothed
by the trigger and
why my life was not
enough to heal it
before hand
found gun.

Parents always say it:
I wish it were me
instead. It could've
been me as well.
We who survive
what takes our
children do not
rest easy.

Hawaiian Language Class

We are walking on the lava
toward the new Kaimu beach.
Kumu Lei is talking,
pointing to things
looking up at the sky
out at the horizon
back at the mountains.
She seems well-located
perfectly aware of her surroundings.
At first, I trail a bit behind her and the group
as I often did on school field trips as a child.

Our kumu pauses occasionally to point things out –
a sturdy little fern growing out of the lava – the
Pele.
"Kupu-kupu" she says, as she points.
Then "ho'opili mai" and we repeat
"kupu-kupu".
She carries on talking and walking.
I keep up better with the walking, of course.
She turns to our small group periodically
"Mai'popo?" She asks if we understand.
At first, I shake my head and say
"A'ole." As my mind and my feet
begin to work together
more often, I am able to say "Ae"

Hawaiian is one of our planet's relational languages.
There are many synonyms, meaning is contextual.
These languages, on a worldwide scale, are not
faring well.
The relationships in question are with the land, sea
and other beings.
And while I don't feel surprised by the overthrow of
relationship,
I feel loss.

I have immigrated to this land that should still be
sovereign.
I want my son to learn Hawaiian.
That's what you do when you
move to a new land and claim
to cherish.
In Hawaii, of course, it's not necessary –
English dominates;
my son will choose for himself.

The language, mana'o and practices of this culture
could be swept away in the tide of globalization –
the tide of economic oppression
scarring the land and polluting the sea as though
human life is not connected to these things.
In English, we have no language for that depth of
connection.
It is easy to forget.
We have lots of words, sure,
but not so it is felt directly in the na'au,
so that it becomes lived experience.

Kumu Lei stops to tell a story about the name of a
place
Nene kahului 'o Kaimu –
the cherished crescent of Kaimu.
Translation is rough because
within the name is a story about land and people,
within that story are many stories about each person
each kumu niu – each coconut tree
planted in this crescent of sand among rocks.

I think how lucky Kumu Lei is to have grown up
with this connection to place and other beings.
Our lives are partly the luck of our birth,
partly a result of where we choose to place our
attention –
each and every day – what we choose to nurture,

what we choose to let perish in the shadow of our
inattention.
Some of us grew up without connection to place –
without a clear role in a community that includes
land and trees,
fish and sea, stars and sky, more –
I worry that we, un-placed, are always in danger
of taking that connection from others
because of our suffering.
This is one root of greed, colonization, profiteering,
a desire to control.
Suffering: having forgotten who we are, in
relationship to all else.

I am reminded of a story about Tecumseh,
a Shawnee who struggled, alongside various tribes,
to resist the transfer of North American land
to the forces of the United States.
Early in the 1800s he met with President Madison
to this aim.
This meeting took place in the nation where I was
born –
on another piece of stolen land.

Using language to establish relationship,
the president's aide instructed Tecumseh
to wait for Madison in this way:
"Sit in this chair, your father will see you now."
To which Tecumseh responded,
"My father is sky. And my mother is the earth,
and I will rest upon her bosom."
Then, he sat on the floor
as the president entered for their talk.
I can only imagine that President Madison,
sitting in his chair, looking down at Tecumseh
might only have seen his relative position of height
might only have thought of his mother as
one small woman,
the instrument of his magnificent birth.

The suffering of the oppressor and
the suffering of the oppressed are
not equal but connected.
Indeed, I suffer each time I allow oppression
and in the moments when I am oppressed
I suffer more greatly when I allow myself
to be defined by others.
Kumu Lei says that naming a place
gives us the responsibility of caring for that place.
As Pele creates new land, new beaches, I feel
grateful
that Lei and her family name these places,
do not let them be defined solely by others.

As we are walking back to the red cinder
of the road beyond the Pele
Kumu Lei talks, looks up at the sky,
which has become cloudy.
"Pehea ke anila?" she asks.
How's the weather? To which I manage:
"He wela." It's hot.
"Polole'i," she says.
Then adds to my correct though simplistic answer,
the nuances of clouds and wind.
I understand, but I couldn't have said it myself.
I have never had the language.

Drought and Urban Wildlife

I.

Descended from the rough and snowless hills
thirsty bears search for lost rivers here
where hoarded water pools in urban sprawl.
Through screen doors, see them back stroke without fear
in concrete ponds, blue light illumines fur.
Watch them as their bodies glide to and fro
and then lie poolside in faux moonlight glow.
They came for the water, not to confer.
But now see them huddle, to make their plans.
It's right to fear that they may have demands.
The lack of rain surely affects them too.
And in the hierarchy of species,
we alone agree we should be on top.
Our arrogant consumption has to stop.

II.

Our arrogant consumption has to stop.
Dried lakes and barren fields make birds fly in
to cities, searching for the moisture there.
From sky they scan each glistening streak
for water, dive our gleaming aqueducts.
So high on arid gusts they must ascend
to fly too far away from nature's tend.
In cities, the sparkle often pretends.
Standing in a fountain, the egret sees
its own reflection in the glass and steel.
Its stringy feathers and too weary wings,
feet shifting among the coins and debris.
Like a last brutal selfie photograph
the birds see their fate, a dry epitaph.

III.

The birds see their fate, a dry epitaph,
as the land mammals too, seek wet relief.
Even those who have long lived among us
find it hard to absorb selfish choices.
With sprinklers off, raccoons struggle to eat.
Like a child who offers a sugar cube
just to watch the creature wash it away,
we laugh at its searching, smile at defeat.
We take perverse joy in using it up,
entitled to water, food, sun and crops.
Seeing only ourselves in this problem,
singing in showers while leaves wilt and drop,
forgetting that we once were mammals too,
descended from the rough and snowless hill.

Empire in Decline

It's just America.
And by that I mean
the country not
the continent which
cannot be fully implicated.

Don't weep and whine,
act so precious in the plight.
Unspoken histories,
hierarchies linger like
seeds traveling on the hem
of a skirt, welt of a shoe.
They'll plant and grow
until what do you know?

America, I am your child.
I grew up strong so
I must've learned to play
and win; I must've learned
the game though I say
I eschew those rules in favor
of sharing and gentleness.
We have all made this America.

It's just America. Don't seem so
serious about its unspooling,
the suffering caused by slack
systems and the stunning speed
with which some new super-power
starts spinning up the skein.

Pele

Aia i hea o Pele?
She lives at Hale'ma'uma'u crater.
Her eyes are red and hot.
She is the mother of land.
Imitate me – she speaks.
Ho'opili mai.
Make yourself big,
fragrant and beautiful.
Put flowers in your black hair.

Each time I visit her
she takes a piece of my flesh
and I grow new.
Sometimes, I think my foolish thoughts:
I don't like to be spoiled
by scratches, cuts and bruises,
somehow, there is
virtue in keeping nice.
She reminds me that
I am made to be torn down
my pride to be shredded,
my false safety to be
gouged blind and
washed away in the tide.
Pele and the laughing sea
make jokes of my
protections, perfections,
possessions of flesh.
She reminds me I heal
get new skin
become new.
Beauty
is in the living.

Possessions

In my Hawaiian language class,
the teacher explained the different
forms of possession possible in Hawaiian.
Each language carries its own mana'o –
the culture has its own meaning.
In Hawaiian, things can belong to you
voluntarily or involuntarily.
Your parents, for example, you didn't choose,
but your children, you chose.
"Some people think children are not a choice –
but they are!" she intoned dramatically.

I made dutiful notes about this distinction
between the use of the words ko'u and ka'u,
though as with most mana'o,
the simplicity of the rule about choice
becomes more complex as the examples mount.
"And it's also like things you don't need – ka'u
versus things you do need – ko'u." She said.
All of the things one can have –
a dishwasher, a Montblanc pen,
the 1920s red upholstered barber chair
in the spare bedroom.
One doesn't need these things. Ka'u.
"A spouse?" somebody asked.
"You gonna be just fine without him."
Our kumu said knowingly.
"Don't need a spouse – you choose it,"
the teacher clarified.

But clothes and places where you sit – ko'u.
She modified the explanation of the rule again.
These are places where you leave part of your mana –
your spirit or life force.
If I were to truly use that barber chair,
my possession of it would change.
She explained that two houses can belong to you –
the one you live in – my house: ko'u hale
the one you built to sell – my house: ka'u hale.
Our kumu is a good teacher.

And I appreciate the varied benefits
of learning a new language, a new culture.
I think of how much of my mana I have left
on lovers, on spouses, on places I have lived
not fully realizing that there was a choice involved,
not fully articulating myself as separate
from so much of what my experience
chooses to possess.

No Victim/No Bully

"I just read a fascinating book about your people –
your part of the world."
And without pausing to know a thing about her
(least not what she thought about this book)
he launched into a series of questions,
mostly statements.
As though he'd already
rounded up a rowdy cadre of facts,
wanted first her congratulations,
for her to fill the gaps
so that he could seem more clever
during his next dinner repartee.

She, from a colonized land,
a group of people
who have been questioned,
examined many times –
why should she help
fill his mind,
give him a shiny ball
to twirl in his idle hands,
perhaps drop it or sell it,
if the timing was right.

Why should she do this;
why does he think his questions benign?
Curious outsiders
are not asking for anything, really.
Not land; not money;
not brides nor slaves nor water rights.
They seek to understand;
understanding is laudable.

They are not asking for anything really –
just information, facts, processes.
They seek to understand.

She offered a few basic phrases
on his chosen subject: her culture.
I thought she didn't say much,
and I think he'd have agreed
because he just carried on:
"I've read about that and it seems to me..."

I watched, listened to his banter,
so divorced from consequence –
he, the famous Irish-American artist.
He, from a colonized land
who could never
oppress another – sought only
to aggrandize himself through
what he could find out.
I watched his entitlement
and marveled, feeling ill,
at how he interrogated
this exceptional woman
whom I was just beginning to know.

And perhaps the queasiness
came from my secondary storyline:
I questioned my own tactics
in my past as an outsider-researcher.
Have I ever been this arrogant?
I'd like to say no, but I can't tell.
He didn't want to know her.
She had some information he could collect,
tasty looking plums he could shake from her tree,
the living tree, a mere utility.

41

But on this night, I learned something.
Nausea quelled as I started
to focus more on her, less on him.
The fruits of her knowledge
did not need the protection
of the ethics committees
or the institutional review boards
that would've tried to regulate
his foolishness, had he really been a researcher
and not an uncouth dinner companion.
She did not need the protection
of committees that sometimes fail anyway
because of the chasm between rules, practice
and American cultural propensity
to look for the loophole,
skirt a rule as a skill,
rather than a deception.
She did not need protection.

I marveled at her skills
recalling that the more useful power
is the power of one's integrity
to make choices about what one will and
won't do; what one will and won't say.
The power to simply not give information,
more useful perhaps than the power
to curtail the questions.
Because once she asserted herself,
he seemed foolish.
He did no harm;
she did not allow it.

She listened politely, turning her coffee cup
in her hands after a fine meal.
She offered minimal information, was polite.
And when she had no further use for his prattle,

his assertions about what he'd read
about her history, she said,
"well, that's not exactly the way it is.
But I don't choose to share
anything further with you about our culture."

"Well, ah, ah, I..."
He stammered for a moment, mouth open,
and my jaw went slack too, thinking
"Oh, hell yes."
I was already looking
for a humorous intervention,
to be clever in that way
that stops a bully without being impolite.
But she did not require intervention –
mine or anyone else's.
And if she was angry,
she didn't show it.
After his stammering, she added,
"Oh, don't take it personally.
My people don't discuss our lives
until the time is right.
And now is not the right time."

She knew about timing.
How many women walk around feeling
we owe anyone an explanation
at any given moment?
How many of us give information to authorities
simply because we've not learned
how to do otherwise.

She knew otherwise.
As I watched his authority uncoil around him,
fall into a heap at his feet,
she just got up and asked
if anyone would like more tea.

Because sassin' the man with the pile of papers bearing your name never got anyone another nickel's worth of health care

She sat looking
at his brown shoes
feeling the
fingertips on
her left hand
with fingertips
on her right
wondering whether
his mama knew
how many people
sat quietly
every day
wishing her
the same poor health
their families faced
while her son
spoke nasty things as he
read and moved
the papers so slowly
across his desk
you'd think college
had stunted his
cognitive ability.
If his mama had
been well and healthy
every day of her life
perhaps the best
and cheapest
healthcare to distribute

to the masses would be
whatever talisman
she fingers in her
housecoat pocket
every time her son
walks through the screen
door and talks
about his work day
with the words
"Those people…"

Dave and His Son (City Heights, 1985)

I am piecing the scene together slowly.
Dave sends his son outside as the white man walks
up the step.
At first, I think he's selling drugs.
The man walks in; sometimes I see the money
pass from hand to hand, as they stand, just inside
the door.
But I don't see what's been exchanged,
no small parcel, something palmed.
My husband and I are the only white people
visible on this block except
the men who come to Dave's apartment.
He sends his nine-year-old son outside when they
arrive.

On a weekend – afternoon through early evening –
they come
about every forty minutes, stay awhile. Sometimes
small
sounds come through the glass jalousie bedroom
window.
Dave tells his son: Go Play and Don't Go Far.
He hangs on wrought iron railings, leans into fence,
watches
as I step out for laundry, or get something from the
car.
I heard Dave tell him once to be afraid of us.
Kid sees me then looks away each time
I turn to see him watching. The white men – always
white –
seem to be sailors: age, walk and haircut.
They look like buyers, mostly ease, some nerves.

I see Dave's wife infrequently as money changes hands.
She's a monument of dark-skinned big-boob-and-booty beauty.
Long straight hair is set into high, big curls. A black Dolly Parton wig.
Tight spandex bodice, short nightie with parted nylon bathrobe.

Dave is cordial toward me when we pass.
I don't ask questions about things that aren't my business and
seem to go quite smoothly, really, except for the kid. I think
about him often. A quiet watcher, hanging on the railing
climbing every possible way up, on and underneath those concrete stairs. I too was told to play outside, but close, in an apartment building about this size. Different reasons. Eavesdropping on neighbors, watching
movements, emotions and affairs – deep lessons on the ways
of adults and culture, as I recall. I fit and flung and hung my body
all the ways against those stairs and metal railings too.
Look busy, always present and soon, no one sees you.
I am learning these neighbors slowly, much as Dave's son
must be learning of the world. But I am no longer invisible.
He stares, then looks away each time I turn to smile.

47

Nearing Adulthood

That first moose was quite a thing to see.
They're large; standing
knee deep in marshy water, whole
landscape seemed bigger still.
My teenage son was unimpressed.
I stopped the car and woke him,
demanding that he gawk,
to which he said emphatically,
"What makes you think I *want*
to see a *moose*?"

Oh, alright then; I was pleased to see one.
So. This waking worked just days before.
Again he'd gone to sleep in irritation
at the vastness of Alaska.
When I woke him: reindeer!
Their gentle noses poking toward
car windows, furry antlers begging touch.
He blinked awake in admiration.

He could not enter two of five hot springs –
too young, they said and so we sat
with children all around looking at
forbidden tranquil waters, bathers with their
eyes closed in repose against the meadow,
tree-lined hill. I threatened to leave
him there, go down the slope myself
if he did not stop acting like a child.
"I'm sorry that fifteen's too young."
He sneered in anger; world's unfair.

I should've woken him for Northern lights.
I would've been asleep myself but I had to
take a walk outside to find the loo.
So late in summer, I thought of LSD
trapped in my cells but no, the greens swirled into
blues
just as in pictures. But he slept warm, untroubled,
by being too old to want this trip,
too young for pleasure in all the world offers.

In an Anchorage mall, I could take no more.
"Just walk around. Here's twenty bucks.
Buy a game; eat cookies. I don't care.
I want a pedicure." He rolled his eyes,
gave me angry face, which I gave back.
"Quit being such a weasel-wang! Why
can't you be a teenager for just an hour in a mall?
I swear…" and on I went until he said,
"Hang on. Did you just call me a weasel's pecker?"

So I had. We laughed and I recall that nail shop's
custom of toe-perfume when painting's done.
"Good god," I thought, and "who's that for?"

My toes smelled nice just for themselves
much as the moose was not superb
for teenage human needs.
Then came berries on a hike,
rivers swelled with fish; we were agog.
And laughing when a woman came unglued
on seeing wolves; she hugged Denali ranger,
bus driver too, a lifelong dream come true.

We both were awed by bears, I think.
I'd always had a mental pic of how their
bush-dining must appear. Somehow tender,
cartoon bears impaling berries, one per claw
but no, one swept its paws through bushes six feet
tall
dove them dripping into maw.
Urgent, gleeful, violence, what I saw.

My son bought me a hat that trip; I have it still.
I was both cold and stubborn in Denali park,
would not purchase what'd been left behind,
though I paused to try it on.
It was my birthday and though he's never
been a gifter (of things like hats)
when we emerged the shop, he pulled it out
and told me "Happy Birthday Mom."

All I Have of Her Are Photos.

My friend Izetta knew
her great-grandmother
and when I wondered how mine got by
she told me the story of hers.
"I knew my great grandmother,"
she said with audible pleasure
at the memory, told me
the story of the sassy woman who
made fear rise in a hot prickle
on your neck to consider speaking
up to her. The woman, though tiny,
could fill space with her presence,
her sharp mouth softening
when confronted with strength.
Izetta spoke back when needed.

All I have of my great-grandmother
are photos and the way my mind
shifts just a bit to another time and place when
I think of her so something of her geography comes
into my throat, makes a little nest there.
Her high yellow skin, by now, looks to be
nothing but sunlight touching mine.
I don't plan it but you can hear small-town
Texas in my voice if you listen for it.

All I have are a few photos
and an erect posture,
something I could've learned
from the length of her neck
in every picture –
she looked upright.

Proud, beautiful, yet comfortable,
gently in control, as though she could hold
her steady gaze
into the camera's eye forever, face relaxed.

She looked as though her hands would never
hold a shotgun to her head
as she heard the music of her children's
laughter – or maybe it was the din
of her baby's crying – after she sent
the older ones outside to play. Out, out.
She sent them out of the house.

How did she do it?
Perhaps her toes were agile, like mine,
feet like hands, one dexterous toe
against the trigger. Or did she pull
the trigger at all? Did anyone wonder?

Ontological Reversal

In which the concept
becomes more important
than the thing itself.

In which children
in poor neighborhoods
are taught to love reading
without ever being
given a book.

In which learning
about photosynthesis
is a leaf-free endeavor.

Orwell warned us
that the language would
double back on itself
meaning-wise, but
did he see the pending
zeal for representations
that no longer conjure
origins? Live performance
becomes video just as
social media becomes
friendship.

Luckily, language conjures.
Put right in the mouth,
it always has.
Poetry, pictures,
plays and prose

verbing all over;
they cannot be
contained by paper.

(*I still long for
pen to paper,
a way to hold you when
your face won't move
with words.*)

The child without the book
can still hold rhythm
in her body. Chapters
in the arms of sunrise,
soft of blanket, breath
of sister, the smiling
teacher, chapter, chapter,
chapter, day by day
a life becomes a
book and more.

Language conjures,
maybe not the leaf itself
but urge to leave the building.

An ontological reversal
can reverse again.
A snap is a movement
with a history – though
pressure on the twig is
harder to see than breakage.

Stories too have history,
show one can
break a promise
without making a promise,
reveal what others
are invested in not seeing.

Poetry is incantation.
Just speak of walls
and walls come up
walls come down,
mortar cakes your
fingernails and your
fences electrify.

When you tell someone
your story, you give them
a part of yourself. When you
see them again, you meet the you
that is in them.
They need not remember
the details, even
the very next day.

That's how we will re-form
a world that can hold
everyone. How we will do what
nature tells us (hopefully)
before it stops
speaking.

Fat Stripper

She tells me she worked
as a stripper for
some time in her youth.
Now middle-aged
she sits comfortably,
laughs easily,
smiles broadly as she
tells me how some
can hate the flower
that does nothing but
its blooming business.

She says even her friends
are angry that she is
still so sexy, despite
the fact that she has
aged and added
fifty pounds
to her small frame.
And even worse,
she does not
torture herself –
as they do –
to have
perfect bodies.
She winks at me
looks me up and down
and smiles
as though we are
in cahoots.

She notes that
I move like
a woman who

knows she's hot,
that women
like us are meant
to stick close
in a world so full
of body shame
and competition.

I have just met her
but of course,
I love her,
because we are sisters
in a family that refuses
to let the neighbors
define our joy,
to trade our treasures
for the infertile plot
of convention
so many are sold.
We are not bound
to barren ideals
of beauty; we are
lush, dirt under
our nails, sun on our skin.

I smile, nod grateful
she recognized me,
called me so quickly
family. As we hug,
her body hums
with life,
with urgency
someone with
joy to spread,
pleasure to celebrate.

1820s French Fashion

When the first giraffe went to France
fashion extended itself.
Women sat on their carriage floors
to accommodate hairdos
held aloft with wire scaffolding.
Hats high in homage
to the elegant neck of the fine creature
who came from the South continent
on a ship rumored to have had a hole
cut through the deck to accommodate
her upright passage from Egypt.

She walked from Marseille to Paris
in forty-one days, wearing stylish boots
and a cape, to parade through throngs
of admirers, 30,000 gathered
in Lyon to see her graceful amble.
The craze lasted only through her youth,
a few years of high hats and hair
of wallpaper and lampshades,
porcelain patterns spotted
like her skin and then she lived
her remaining eighteen French years
as part of the royal menagerie,
never saw another like herself again.

If she were making her stroll today
would the paparazzi cause her to stumble
in her even taller boots; would
images of her loveliness show an even longer
airbrushed neck? Would we extend her
eyelashes and cap her teeth, leave her looking

to a sky void of leaves to preserve her
girlish figure in a landscape lacking companions?
Would we romanticize her peerlessness,
distorting what we admire until
it can do nothing but admire us back?
Sad consolation for the isolation it takes to be
a thing of beauty, so long ago
removed from home.

Modern Civilization

There is a woman examining a shoe.
This is a familiar scene.
It would be hard to explain why
a shoe requires examining, and yet
she seems content and this seems normal.
You are not imagining her examining
a shoe for its sturdiness as if
preparing for a long journey; neither
do you imagine her examining the origin
of something sharp or rough.
This shoe has not been worn; it is new.
You know this when you hear that
a woman is examining a shoe.

It's not quite 11 a.m. and the shoe
is in her hand; the store is not long open
and there she stands. She cocks her head
and looks at the heel – from the bottom
from the side; she examines the shoe.
It has a high heel. To examine
the shoe at this hour precludes it being
comfortable. That shoe would need
a quick slip on, a walk around, a tidier
consideration, but not an examination.

Before lunch, the woman is considering
her place in modern civilization,
in a world that offers her identities
in which glamour and shoes like these
will be required, rewarded. There will be
discomfort, but nothing resembling
a long walk, a sharp stone, sturdy wear.
This discomfort will be self-imposed

so the examination is a meditation of sorts
in her otherwise irksome day.
Her mind casts peace, light into shadow,
when she tries on an identity
worthy of adoration, stares.
Being cared for carries
a certain power. She needs a boost
before this day has fully begun,
let alone rounded the noonday curve.
She is momentarily content, breathing easy.
There is a woman examining a shoe.

Genetic Lottery

I had a lover who'd say,
"Baby, you are so gorgeous!
You're just not like other women.
They can't help it.
You won the genetic lottery, that's all –
your eyes, your hair!
People pay money for lips like yours,
cleavage like yours."

I felt rewarded
as people do, I suppose,
when they win the lottery.
It's chance, sure,
but quickly becomes proof
that I merit rewards.

Then she left me for another woman
and said of her new lover,
"She's just so gorgeous!
It's different than with *you*."
As though it would mean nothing to me,
she said,
"I was never attracted to *you*, anyway..."

Today's lottery winner has been chosen.
In my lover's pocket is only one prize
because for a while,
I was no longer rich.
I could've looked to the pocket
of another lover-daddy-millionaire
but something was changing in me.

I felt sorry for myself for losing,
sorry for myself and the new winner
knowing how worthless the prize really is.
I felt pity for my lover
who really has no prize to give
if she needs others to prove
she's gorgeous too.

But with that love so long ago, it seems
pity is only due for the game itself
seeking energetic revenues of players like us.
I focus on my own fortune,
no longer buying a ticket.

Hungry Tiger Behind a Flimsy Picket Fence

My girlfriend conducts a running dialogue with age.
Age doesn't show up
for the conversation, most times.
It doesn't need to.
She has monologue to last for days,
prepared requests that don't wait for response.
Still, she asks for a waylaying
of the loose skin on her thighs,
offers to make age's bed every day for a month
if she can postpone the arrival
of any pinchable skin
on her trim, firm belly.

She regales age with tales of sporting conquests.
Her smiling innocence is winsome;
it's no wonder that age treats her delicately.
She looks positively girlish some days –
soft skin, smooth across her abrupt little nose,
hair flouncing around her elegant neck.
Still, she quietly worries
about the warm flowering of menopause,
her assumption of looming dementia.

I am younger, though not by much.
Each comment I make hears the retort
"Easy for you to say!"
Age is like a hungry tiger,
behind a flimsy picket fence.
She spends so much time
standing on the sidewalk, taunting, cajoling;
she's bound to sustain damage one day.
Age may be voracious at times, but I choose

not to look it in the eye for too long at a stretch,
give it courteous respect, but nothing more.
I walk on to the next yard,
leave that cat to its pacing.
There are peonies to enjoy in the next yard,
besides.

Parting, Renewal

1. Parting

We have reached the impasse
where moving and staying both seem futile.
We change because we cannot see the way to do
other.
We move because the ground beneath us does,
and we do not know how
to cleave more tightly to it.
This is a time of looking away
from each other's faces,
letting our eyes rest on headlines
of newspapers at adjacent tables.
This is the time of broken promises,
realizing the ones we should've made
to ourselves. The thousand little
lies of our days
have laid their eggs like flies
on the sweet fruit for which we hunger.

2. Renewal

We have destroyed the sweet, irrational security
of our previous lives.
To our surprise spring brings
wildflowers to the once
shifting, breaching ground.
Choices sit as simply and weightily
as a morning-orange papaya
on a blue breakfast plate.
All edges are crisper,

colors more distinct.
Morning glories creep
in a field well turned and cleared of mines.
I laugh with joy and comfort,
unsure what will happen after the pen is laid away.
Now is the time for steeping tea, looking out the window,
smelling the newly dug earth with gratitude.

In This Body

In this body, a river flows.
Pelvic bowl of sunshine spills
over landscape and the heart
basks, a reed rooted
in marsh-mud, twisted,
whistling in wind.

The knowledge that shimmers
in this landscape is not nestled
in the head like a burrow,
like a hibernation cave,
like a tree hollow,
hiding nuts for winter.
In this body, vessels abound.
The skull is a sturdy bowl,
the liver a flask;
kidneys swell like sponge.
Knowing emanates from
everything, mixes everything
in a frisson of alive alert aloud.
In this body, there is always
movement; even in stillness,
the breath animates; cells inhale.

This body contains a river
married to a river.
Someone composed a
song for the wedding of self
and self flowing into self.
Everyone turned out
for the ceremony and smiled
on the spectacle.

In this body, wet movement
brings peace and furious change,
pushing like birth, bones
softening, separating
giving way to life that is
both same and different, of
this body yet unique.
Wet movement brings peace and fury.
Rest and sleep fill
the reservoirs between vertebrae
fill the pools in the corners
of eyes and spill saliva
onto pillow and sheets,
moisten fascia like dew.

The river shrinks and swells
turns land to water allowing
it to remain.
The river knows melt,
shine, swish and move,
move, move.
The river knows itself as
companion, carnally and
carefully, not always capable
of holding its own gaze,
touching its wondering face.
There is no moment when
the river recedes entirely
in this body.

Water is waiting
in its sun-cloak, frost-cloak
married, moving,
waiting,
just as wet.

Turns Out My Wife is Bipolar

How can one be angry at a helpless person
who photographs her own feet more often
than looking loved ones in the eyes?
She consumed the kitchen table rather
than working at her own desk, in her own
room; she shared every room with me –
poor little fucker – until I had nothing
of my own and still, she felt she had less.
How can one be angry with one who needs care?
I was.

Not at first. I made a shield of my body,
a pillow of my body, a rope of my body
to drag her out of the house when she
couldn't bring herself to move. "Let's
get that nice Turkish coffee you like.
Let's go. C'mon. Nice little walk."
I used all of me, dragged her up,
never heard thanks and this was fine
until it wasn't. It never worked; then
the rope of me hung limp and I grew
nervous at the way she eyed me,
determined to use me to do herself harm.
In the beginning it was easy to take
care, temporary. I loved her and was
beloved.

At what point did I become angry
not to be loved by a person who took
on the task, made the vow and yet
seemed never to make it a priority?
During the days when it was always dusk

and I wondered if I'd find her sitting
in the same chair when I left home
and arrived back, wondered if I'd find
her breathing or slumped over her computer,
hanging in the kitchen from some fixture
I'd have never guessed would bear her
weight – during those days, she loved me
like a raft after shipwreck. What good is
a raft if you never find land? (And saving
someone's not the same as being seen, is it?)
I shaped my life around her stated desires,
though she could do nothing for herself
but state them. I laid the plans and told
the stories to prompt her better life, her
laughter.

Her body was tense when she
let me touch it. One night,
I ordered her to bed, told her to take off the
clothes she sometimes wore for days,
sleeping and waking. She felt like one giant
muscle. "Face down," I said. Her eyes darted,
jaw tensed and the neighbors chatted,
in Spanish, two beers in, on their front porch.
This often comforted her somehow.
As I rubbed her back with coconut oil,
nothing released but her humor and she said,
"Why do I resist you?" I said, "I don't know."
"I always think you mean to hurt me," she said.
"I mean to soothe you," I answered.
"Okay then. Could you put a little more of that
goat's blood you're smearing me with
on my shoulders? I think it feels good."
"Yes, of course."

Maybe I knew it at first: that I could not
be happy without her happiness. Perhaps
that's what made me urgent, earnest in her care.
So much that my jaw tightened, eyes darted too.
Like a child with discontented parents who
rarely saw approving glances, despite the efforts
I made. No matter how I planned to please them
they would not be made whole and happy. Though
I grew up, healed up, made my peace, my home,
alone,
I am fine, but with someone? I am not like that
child,
I am her.

How can one turn ruthless in the face of
inability, helplessness, woe and regret?
Not even basic kindness and civility in the end.
Poor thing couldn't help what she was saying.
Though it was true, it's ruthless too, to be cast
as the cause of pain, and watch it become all
she was.

Once we'd bound our lives together, lashed
ourselves to the mast as the motor of marriage
carried us on, the quotidian pain of insanity's
song challenged both of us, her life,
me too.

Everywhere We Go

The bus ride makes you peaceful.
You're getting somewhere, riding,
sleeping, listening to music,
taking a picture of a streetlamp
in the rain, your feet on the grey,
mottled floor, brightened by
dirty pink gum and your laces.

I will be the woman who sits near you
and talks about visiting my son
in prison, how I will always love
him even though he hasn't done right.
You will appreciate the soft sadness
of my eyes and my love for him.
You will write about me later.

I will be the boy with a toy car
who looks at you like a peer when
you twinkle in your smiling voice, say
"Well hello. Where are you going?"
I will reply, "To the same place
as you because we're on the same bus!"
You will laugh and say, "Yes,
of course that must be so."

I will sit next to you at the Hardees
rest stop, notice your dismay
with the black coffee in your hands.
You will inform me that they don't
have half and half, only the white powder
and you've learned that lesson before.
I will think how kind you look,

and lost, somehow hopeful but sad.
I will offer you french fries.

When you take them and say,
"These are shit,
but I love them," it will be like you
are giving me a gift, though
I'm the one who's given you
something and I will ache.
I can't think of anything else I have to give.

The Trap

The barnacles I understood immediately.
Cling to something solid that stays in motion.
Let it move you.

The lobster's faulty logic seems to bring it death.
What was it looking for?
Get in the box, but not back out.

That's cement globbed in the bottom.
It looks like just the barnacles.
A strange shape of heavy, tied with rope.
The lobster can get in, but not out.

How did the human first figure that
ropes tied just so would both entice
and entrap? Once known,
what let them make the box again and
again, pile them high on the dock
in the pink sunset?

It's easy to feel sorry for the lobsters.
Their sad sweetness in butter
prompts tools of murder.
But the barnacles die just as surely,
despite their ingenuity.

Leavers and Stayers

When you come from leavers,
you learn to leave.
If only it were that simple.

The thing is, it's possible,
probable, to come
from one leaver and one clinger,
one parent – often the woman –
who holds on despite reason
to leave, despite lies or bruises
despite the money spent
despite her own children
unsafe in their beds.

Maybe you come
from a mother
who is a leaver-stayer
who stays with one man
after another when she really
should leave and then she leaves
only to find the next.
Maybe it's not her at all,
but your father who wants to
leave and just can't disturb
his collars, comfortable
in the corner closet.

Maybe you come from a leaver
who stays in body and leaves
in other ways; there are many
ways to leave a family, leave
them without smiling, without talking,
without money, love or hope.

Maybe your parents left but stayed,
both of them. That could happen.
Or they left for real and
regretted as people do, who say
they're sorry and still can't
manage to behave any
differently than they do.

It'd be handy to isolate
the cause of your painful ways
to leavers and stayers
who planted a hundred
small expectations that,
though their roots descended,
could be tugged up diligently
through self-help and therapy
and yoga and workshops and drugs.
The way we hold our love
and errors, expectations and
responses are tangled, and rooted
into common ground; that's how
we find each other and become capable
of doing what we feel we must do.

Keep Dancing
(for Pulse Nightclub)

"Dance like the bullet is your heart."
Daphne Gottlieb

Keep dancing.
Take turns carrying
the stone of grief.
Take turns watching
the door for trouble.
Keep dancing.
Take turns holding
up the banner
of celebration,
the bodies of
the dead and wounded.
Keep dancing.
Keep loving.
Keep fucking
and shouting out
the joy of the
body's beating
heart. Take turns
lying down to
rest and breathe
easy. Take turns
lying down to
hold one another,
in the sunshine
in the neon, in the
water and cool air.
Keep welcoming
the strangers in
while the music

plays. Watch the
door for those
who need disarming,
need dancing, need
rest, need loving.
Take turns believing
that only good
can come to those
who are faithful
to the beat,
the ecstasy,
the welcome.
Keep dancing.
Do your part in
the call and response
of hearts beating
breath moving.
Take turns believing
when faith is lost.
Keep dancing.

A Crescent of Sand

I went to the shores of my mind where I could see
myself, by moonlight, digging,
scooping sand
with my fingers, palms
pressed full of the cold, damp heaviness.

Next to the sea, in that place where the sand
is wet, but dry, packed
down a few feet away
from the moving water, I dug out
a crescent two feet deep, large
enough to hold the shape
my body makes when it sobs.
Alone, beneath moonlight, I cried.

It's unlikely that I dug, but
the body carries its own memory.
There has been a lot of sand
under my nails in this life.
The body says sand.
It says ocean held you.
It says, trust me. I have
looked after you before.

I didn't know how damaged I was,
how sane I was for being so damaged.
Maybe it's truer
to say this: other people
didn't know.
I didn't know how well I was taking care
of myself: the drugs, the sex, the over-eating,
the under-eating, the writing,

the long walks at night,
the way I made a place for the earth
and sea to hold me like a mother.

The geography
of my infrequent embodiment replays,
even now sometimes, I travel
according to the landscape of my mind.
The body follows actual geography
in lapsed landscape.

When I was broken,
the body and the mind
made a plan to mend me.
They didn't tell me what they were doing.
They worked, cheerfully in secret,
asking for help when they had to.
Finally, I was well enough to know.
In thanks, I give them all the love and precious
things I can.

If you want to get out of something,
let your mind make a door.
Let your body walk through it.
The other way around works equally well.

When the Horror of the Past Plays Back

You live beyond it.

The body folds itself
into new shapes.

Your mouth grows
new words it didn't
know to speak before.

Your fertile throat
won't hold silence
like it did;
there's too much
life mulching, seeds
splitting.

Then the past lassos you
and you didn't see it coming, dismissed
what seemed inconsequential: sound
of speeding rope
until it constricted across your skin
ripping and pulling you
into submissive
shapes, lungs tight,
knees grinding gravel,
bowing, flesh bulging around restraint,
tears choking words.
You feel you must
make the shapes and sounds
of shame, defeat.

But the more there is to your life
over time, the more varied shapes
your body has.
The rope is made
of feathers;
the past tickles you
makes you want to laugh and
show your seeming assailants gratitude.
The past lassos you with stars;
you've swallowed constraint
as well as the cosmos,
learned to cell-speak with soupy earth and solid,
with core and circumference – your home.

You have lived beyond.

Soon, the past contains more than pain.
You are vast and complex with tales of glory,
gore and fine fabrics against your
scarred skin.
So many solitary sunsets
in your past you remembered,
all you are.

I Chronicle Ephemera for the Museum of Desire

The museum of desire has no doors;
there's always a gentle breeze
in the long corridors, caressing the vaulted ceilings.
The museum of desire is open.
It looks empty and yet, as we walk
its long hallways, experiencing sweet air,
cool stones beneath our feet,
the exceptional quality of light, at once
hazy and bright, clear and distinct,
an illumination beyond longing sets in.
Everything we never lost is tucked
within the walls
reminding us that wanting means life.
Greed for the next breath is good –
still one can learn to breathe easy.
Even in the morning, at noon, and dusk
the light, perfect.
The museum looks empty and miraculously
as we forgive lack,
we become utterly full.

Love and Beauty

Each day presents something new and fleeting
on which to exercise the muscle of love.

We cannot contain the love we have already
received. It is spilling out of our pores,
soaking the ground like spring.

How can there still be wrongs to forgive?
We practice gratefully,
taking in words broken by pain and anger
and restoring them to wholeness.
With so much practice,
we will never forget this skill.

Gather where your beauty is irrelevant.
So much writhing, magnificent joy surrounds you,
how could your loveliness matter?

Become part of the sparkling crowd,
all of you, doing beauty like breathing,
sweating pretty from your pores,
shaking it onto the humming earth.

The sea was wearing its iridescent blue taffeta frock
today,
crinkled with wind, a grey sash around its horizon,
sunlight pressing dimples into its cheeky smiles.
I was surrounded,
resplendent in my insignificance.

Acknowledgments

Seriously though.

Poetry is an act of love, not as well-respected as it should be for its ability to re-create the world. Poetry is an incantation and people don't usually get paid that much for that.

Thanks to Ted Washington for committing to publish poetry, year after year, little by little. You put art into the world, including this book. Bless you.

Thanks to the residencies that support people who write poetry. Vermont Studio Center gave me a month of time to focus on writing poetry in 2006. I also spent time working on this poetry at Dickinson House and Summer Arts in 2015. Residencies have allowed me not only to focus on writing, but to discuss it with other artists, to make sense of the writing and how it moves in the world.

Thanks for making this book look good Toni Le Busque, Rebecca Rubenstein, Cara Weston and Samantha Fields, with your cover design, editing and cover art. Thanks to Kumu Lei and Kumu Loke for their efforts in teaching me Hawaiian, though I'm a slow learner. I'm grateful.

Thanks to all the poets I've ever known, heard and read. Every single one of you. I didn't learn to write poetry in school, I went to poets and places where hard and beautiful life make the breath shorter, the spaces between the words longer and the ability to choose language all the more important. I'm still learning, still teaching, still guided by love and need.

Previously Published

Poetic Inquiries of Reflection and Renewal, 2017
"Modern Civilization"
"Resignation to Fashion"

Nimrod International Journal, 2016
"All I Have of Her Are Photos"

Heart Journal (Human Equity through Art), 2013
"Love and Errors"

So to Speak: A Journal of Feminist Thought and
Literature, 2013
"1820s French Fashion"

Dangerous Sweetness, 2013
"Rest"

Women's Comedic Arts as Social Revolution, 2012
"The Story He Can Understand" (abridged)

San Diego Poetry Annual, 2008
"Parting, Renewal"